How God Speaks to You

How God Speaks to You

by
Mary Soliel

12 ✦ 12
Productions

Santa Fe, New Mexico

How God Speaks to You

Copyright © 2020 by Mary Soliel

All rights reserved. No part of this book may be used
or reproduced by any means without
the written permission of the publisher.

Twelve Twelve Productions, LLC books may be ordered
through booksellers or Amazon.com.

Twelve Twelve Productions, LLC
P.O. Box 22333
Santa Fe, New Mexico 87502

www.marysoliel.com
alighthouse@mac.com

ISBN: 978-1-7362311-4-2

For all
beautiful children
who seek God's
magical signs...
for YOU!

God creates all of life, and can speak to you through signs… or s y n c h r o n i c i t y.
Now that is One Big Word!

Signs are little miracles that happen every day. They give us messages of love, happiness, laughter, and often guide us.

God's special messengers are the angels. Just as our God sends us signs, our angels send us signs too. We each have loving angels who watch over us!

It is all very magical.

God and your angels say "I love you" in so many ways. It may be through a heart-shaped cloud.

Or a heart-shaped cactus. Don't touch or "Ouch!"

You may even receive a love sign from a sudsy pan when helping Mom or Dad with the dishes. There are so many ways to receive signs.

God may speak through a wild animal that you suddenly see, sometimes right near the road. This elk wants you to know that great things are ahead.

The buffalo reminds us to be grateful for all that we have. All animals have a message to give. Put your hand on your heart and feel their message.

God may even speak through pictures that make you smile. Dolphins are all about joy.

Sometimes a little being may appear just to say "Hi there, my friend!"

God often speaks through clouds. Do you see an animal's head in this cloud?

Sometimes it looks like someone is waving at you from up there. Clouds are so much fun to watch!

God likes to speak through rainbows, to remind you that everything will be okay.

God speaks through beautiful sunrises and sunsets. People love to just sit and enjoy the colors. Can you find the flying pelican?

God likes to find ways to make you laugh. Even through a potato head, to cheer you up when you're feeling a bit sad.

God may speak through amazing rocks. Do you like to hunt for rocks and find treasures? What does this rock look like? Can you give it a "high five"?!

Sometimes you come across a rock that makes you smile as big as the Grand Canyon. Let's see the biggest smile you can make.

God speaks through a coin (or coins) left on the sidewalk or on the beach. Pick it up, it's for you!

What if you come across a blue-eyed pelican who sits perfectly still for a picture? "Wow weeeee!"

God may speak through an insect that hangs out with you...

... or near you. They sometimes look right at you. Isn't that cool?!

Or you may receive a sign by finding a ladybug in your hair. Now that is lucky!

Often, you'll see them right on your path, which is always extra special. That means it's for you to see. Just watch your step.

God may speak through colorful sun rays all over your face.

A parent can take a picture with the sun behind you, if you'd like. You must not look right at the sun, though. So ask a parent to capture it.

God speaks softly through the sun and its rays.

God can speak loudly through bold and beautiful colors on the land and sea.

God speaks through all of nature in endless ways.

Even through God's happy (rain drop) tears. Can you find a heart shape or a funny face created from these happy tears?

God so often speaks through numbers. Did you see the numbers 444 today? The number 444 is a very special sign of *the power of God's love.*

When you see the same 3 numbers together—on a license plate, a road sign, or you catch it on the clock—it's extra lucky. You may find 111, 222, 333, 444, 555, 666, 777, 888, or 999!

Maybe it's a sign that you will take a fun new class or make a new friend. Or something really special and exciting will happen. Make a wish!

When you are in the car, it's especially fun to look at license plates, signs, trucks, and everywhere for the numbers. This is a great car game!

Did you see 3 of the same numbers in a row, anywhere today? Or even 2 of the same, such as 77, that's lucky too. If not today, maybe tomorrow!

God speaks to parents in all of these very same ways. But this is a book created just for you. God has a very special love for all children, as you may feel a very special love for God.

You can talk to God just like you talk to your very best friend. You can ask God for help with any problems or worries. Or just say "Hello, dear God." God wants you to be happy, and signs sure can make you extra happy.

God is here for you every day. "Thank you, God," in return, you may wish to say.

www.ingramcontent.com/pod-product-compliance
Lightning Source LLC
Chambersburg PA
CBHW041544040426
42446CB00003B/222